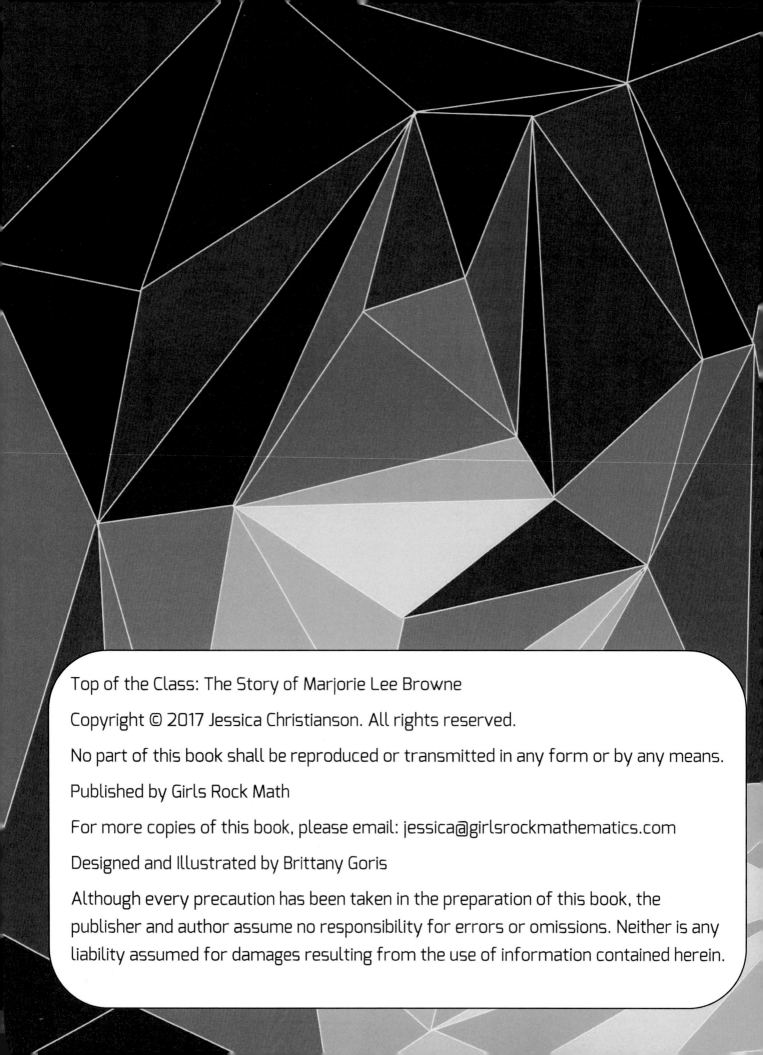

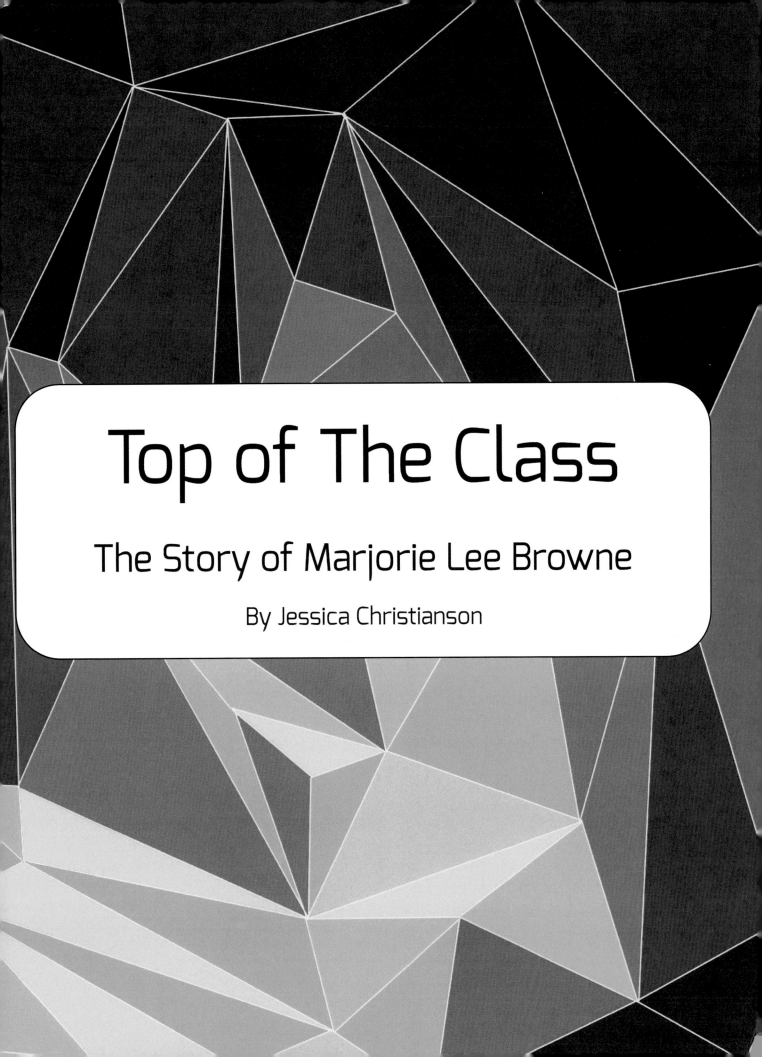

# Top of The Class

## The Story of Marjorie Lee Browne

By Jessica Christianson

A place can change a lot in one hundred years. The United States has changed in many ways since the early 1900s.

One hundred years ago, most people didn't own a car or a kitchen stove, and half of the people in the United States lived on a farm.

One hundred years ago, life was very different for children. If you were a child living one hundred years ago, you might have worked in a factory! You might work six days a week, for eighteen hours a day, just to earn one dollar. Kids as young as six years old could work in a factory using dangerous machines.

**Think About it!**

Why do you think people were worried that children were not safe working in the factories?

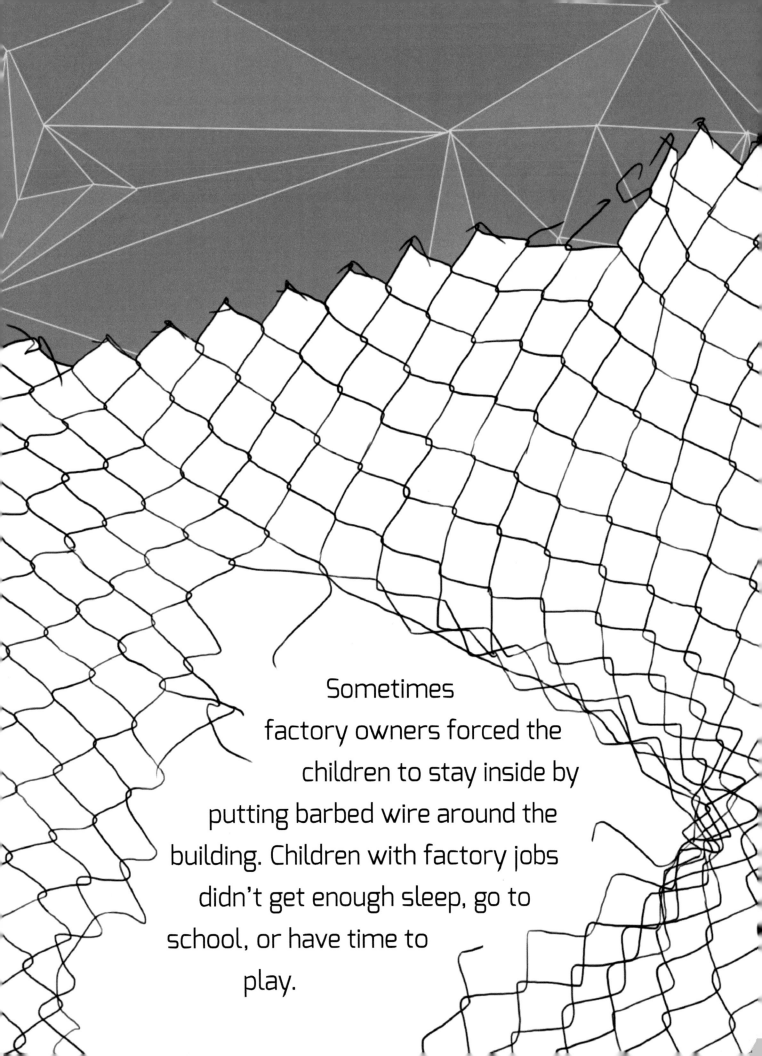

Sometimes
factory owners forced the
children to stay inside by
putting barbed wire around the
building. Children with factory jobs
didn't get enough sleep, go to
school, or have time to
play.

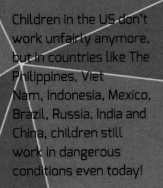

Children in the US don't work unfairly anymore, but in countries like The Philippines, Viet Nam, Indonesia, Mexico, Brazil, Russia, India and China, children still work in dangerous conditions even today!

# DOWN WITH CHILD LABOR

But times were changing. Many people thought it was cruel to force children to work so hard. People got together to take a stand against the factory owners. They wanted all children to get a chance to go to school, play, and live a healthy life.  It took many years to outlaw child labor, but now it is illegal for children to have those kinds of jobs in the United States.

One hundred years ago life was very different for women. If you were a woman living back then, you probably couldn't imagine being a doctor, a scientist or a lawmaker. Most women stayed home and cared for the family. It was a common idea that "a woman's place is in the home." But times were changing.

Susan B. Anthony (right) and Elizabeth Cady Stanton (left)

Women such as **Susan B. Anthony** and **Elizabeth Cady Stanton** worked hard to help women get the right to vote in the United States.  These women were called Suffragettes.

**Think about it!** Is voting an important right? Why do you think women wanted to be able to vote so badly?

Other changes were happening as well. During this time, there were lots of "firsts" for women: first female doctor, first female dentist, architect, US Representative, and more. More women were going to college. Women wanted to be treated equally.

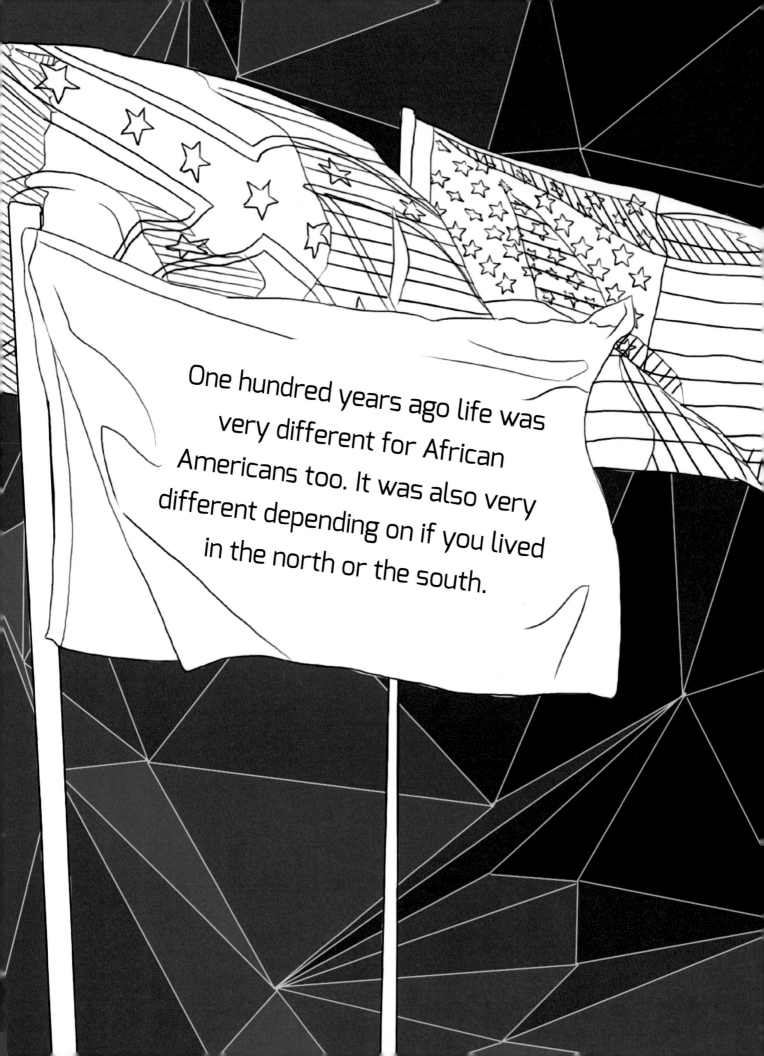

One hundred years ago life was very different for African Americans too. It was also very different depending on if you lived in the north or the south.

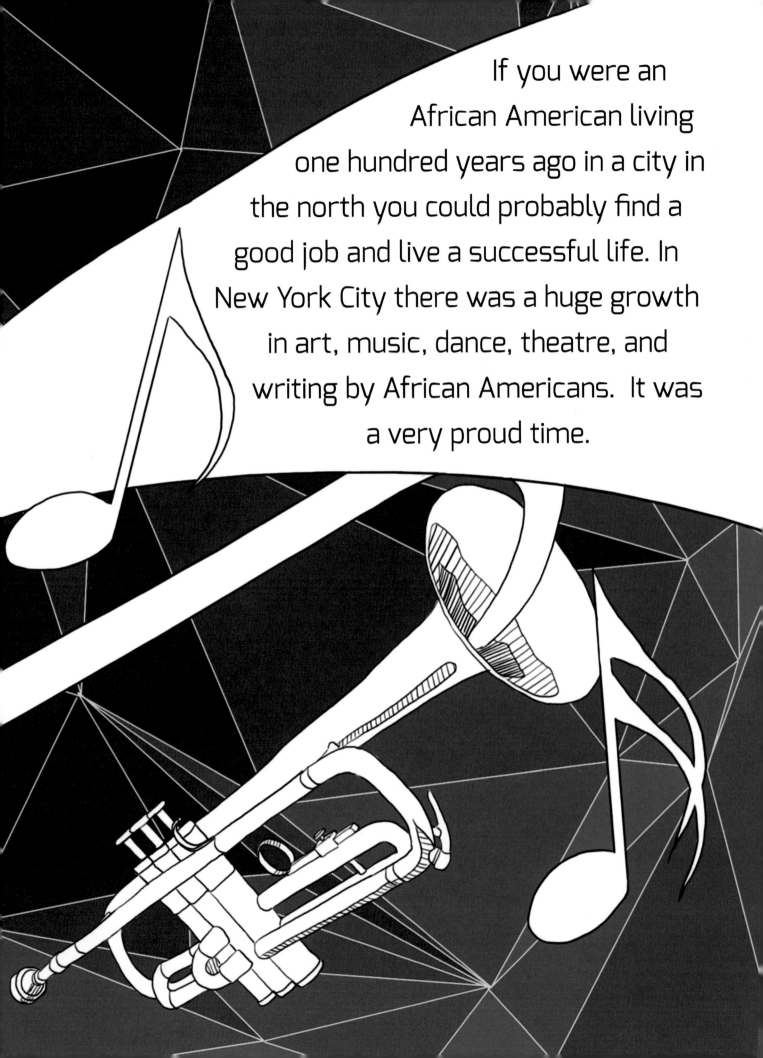

If you were an African American living one hundred years ago in a city in the north you could probably find a good job and live a successful life. In New York City there was a huge growth in art, music, dance, theatre, and writing by African Americans. It was a very proud time.

If you were an African American living in the south however, it would be hard to find a good job and you would not have very much freedom. **Jim Crow Laws,** or laws that claimed it was okay for things to be "separate but equal," were very unfair. African Americans could not use the same pools, movie theaters, restaurants, shops, bathrooms, and even drinking fountains as white people.

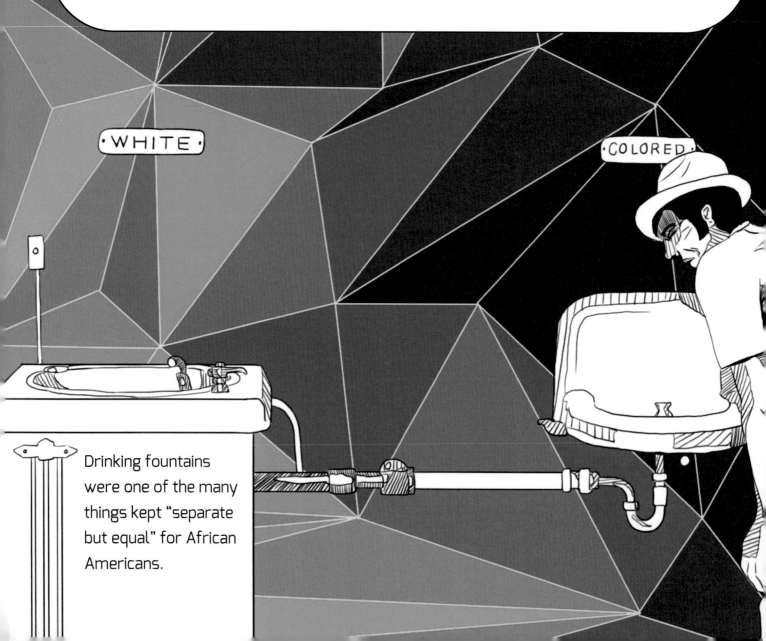

·WHITE·

·COLORED·

Drinking fountains were one of the many things kept "separate but equal" for African Americans.

It took many people working very hard for over sixty years to desegregate the south. Civil Rights leaders like **Dr. Martin Luther King Jr.** and **Rosa Parks** helped change these laws.

Dr. Martin Luther King Jr.

This was the world Marjorie Lee Browne was born into in 1914. Children were fighting for their rights, women were fighting for their rights, and African Americans were fighting for their rights. Born in Memphis, Tennessee on September 9th, Marjorie entered a world that was unfair in many ways.

Did that stop her? No! Marjorie wouldn't let any obstacle get in her way.

Marjorie's father was a math whiz and loved to be quizzed by his friends and family. He would often do mental arithmetic problems for fun. He taught Marjorie and his other children to love math. Here's one of his favorite math tricks that you can try:

Think of a number below 10.

Double the number, then add 6 to the number you have now.

Half the answer, that is divide it by 2.

Subtract your original number.

What do you get?

Even when Marjorie was a little girl, she could see the unfairness all around her. She remembered seeing all of the white children lining up for school outside of a brand-new building as she and her siblings walked to the old school building filled with old books.

Marjorie's parents always encouraged her to try hard and to work hard. At first, when she saw something that looked challenging, she would feel nervous and scared. Then she would tell herself, "I can do it!" She would keep trying even if she felt like giving up.

Marjorie would raise her hand in school, even if she wasn't sure her answer was right. If her teacher asked for a student to volunteer, Marjorie would go up to the board even if she was scared. This helped Marjorie learn more and become confident.

Why is it sometimes hard or scary to raise your hand in class?

Marjorie's father wasn't a rich man, but he had a good job working for the post office.

Her parents saw that she was incredibly hard working and very bright. She loved learning.

She told them, "I can change the world if I just learn how."

So they worked hard to send her to a better school.

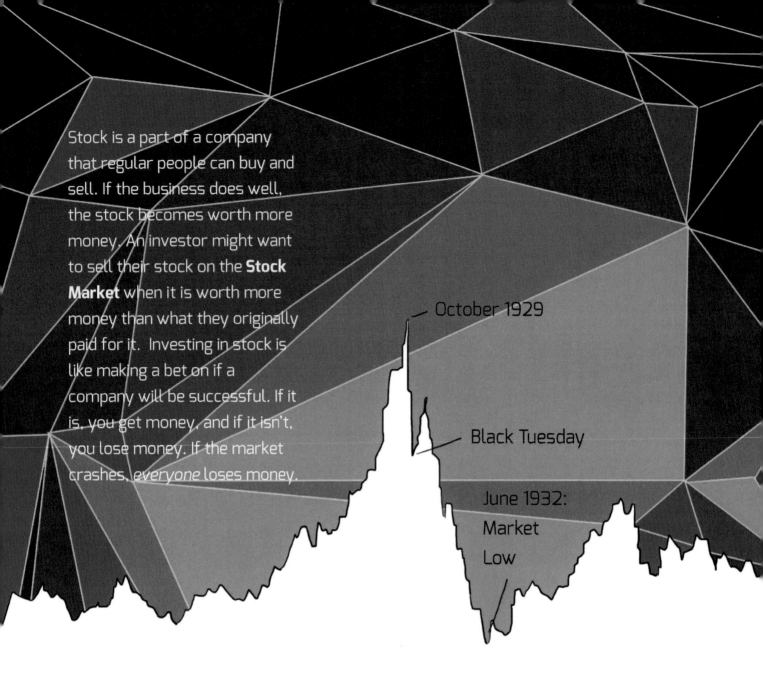

Stock is a part of a company that regular people can buy and sell. If the business does well, the stock becomes worth more money. An investor might want to sell their stock on the **Stock Market** when it is worth more money than what they originally paid for it. Investing in stock is like making a bet on if a company will be successful. If it is, you get money, and if it isn't, you lose money. If the market crashes, _everyone_ loses money.

October 1929

Black Tuesday

June 1932:
Market
Low

Then, in 1929 something terrible happened in America: the stock market crashed, and suddenly people everywhere lost their jobs. Families were starving, people lost their houses, and it was the hardest time that many people had ever faced. They called this **The Great Depression**.

Marjorie knew she would have to be inventive to make a success of herself now!

There was no extra money for her parents to help with college, but she was determined to graduate anyway. During the Great Depression when people had so little money, going to college was a luxury. But it came with hard work.

An unemployed citizen searching for work

Marjorie worked hard in college. She not only studied hard, but she had a job in a diner on the weekends.

In 1935 she graduated cum laude* with a degree from Howard University in math. She had done it! She had really made her parents proud! More importantly, she was proud of herself!

*Cum laude means "with distinction"

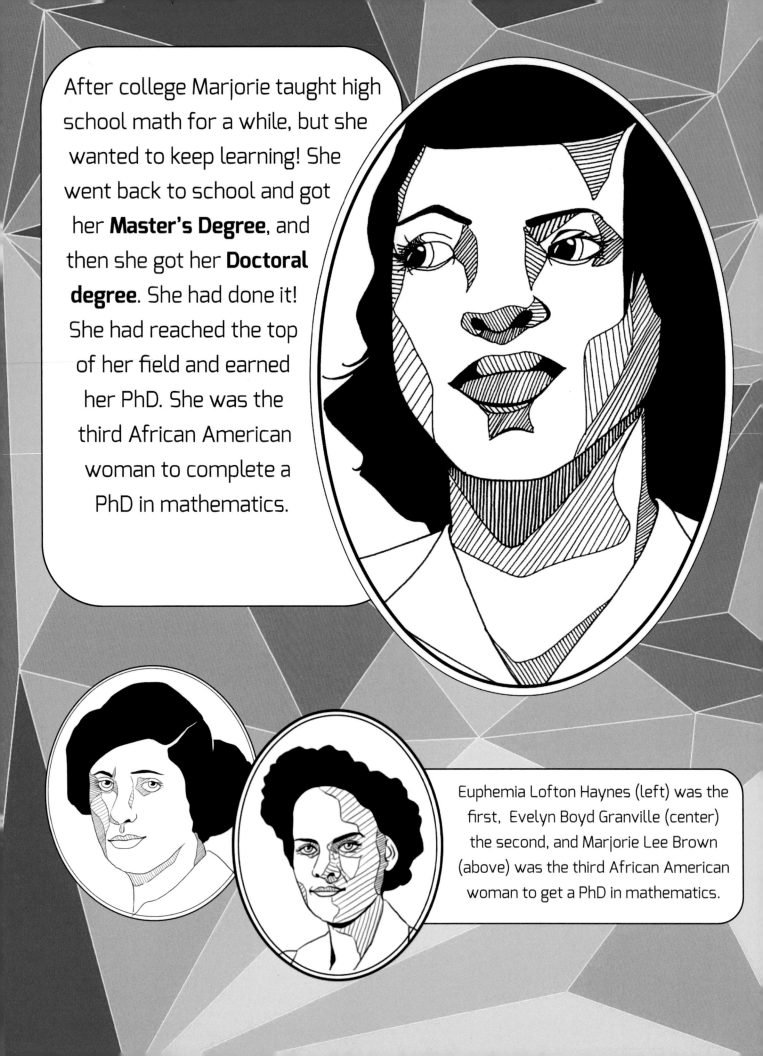

After college Marjorie taught high school math for a while, but she wanted to keep learning! She went back to school and got her **Master's Degree**, and then she got her **Doctoral degree**. She had done it! She had reached the top of her field and earned her PhD. She was the third African American woman to complete a PhD in mathematics.

Euphemia Lofton Haynes (left) was the first, Evelyn Boyd Granville (center) the second, and Marjorie Lee Brown (above) was the third African American woman to get a PhD in mathematics.

When Marjorie was a college professor, she never forgot what it meant to work hard. Seeing so many people struggle, fight for their rights, and overcome challenges made her a very strong woman. When her students struggled financially, she would let them do odd jobs around her house. She

would make sure they had the money they needed for their books or school fees. She was a wonderful teacher and was very admired by all who knew her.

Marjorie was well loved by her students

Marjorie studied a field of mathematics called **TOPOLOGY.** Topology is really fun! If we imagine surfaces to be made of clay, any kind of bending, mushing, and shaping you do to it without tearing, punching holes, or gluing can be described by topology. The number of holes in an object is a property that will stay the same if moved in a very special way.

A favorite example is a clay doughnut which can be smoothly manipulated into the shape of a coffee mug. The doughnut hole becomes the coffee cup handle so that the number of holes is preserved. The doughnut and the coffee mug therefore have the same topology. What fun could you have exploring topology with a hunk of clay?

Another fun way that you can explore topology is with a **Möbius strip**!

# Timeline of Marjorie Lee Browne's Life

* 1914 Marjorie is born in Memphis, Tennessee

* 1920 Women get the right to vote in the United States

* 1929 Stock Market crash starts the Great Depression

* 1935 Marjorie graduates with a BA in mathematics from Howard University

* 1938 The Fair Labor Standards prohibits child labor

* 1939 Marjorie gets her Masters in Mathematics

* 1939 The Great Depression ends

* 1949 Marjorie begins teaching at North Carolina College

* 1950 Marjorie earns her PhD in Mathematics

* 1960 Marjorie brings the first IBM computer lab to her college, the first for any majority African-American University

* 1968 The Jim Crow era in the South finally ends

* 1979 Marjorie Lee Browne Dies

## Discussion Questions

★ What are some ways people in the past changed the world so that people have more rights and freedoms today?

★ Do you think facing obstacles helps someone or hurts someone?

★ What are some ways people have changed things that they see as unfair?

# Afterword

Have you ever heard someone say, "Knowledge is power?" What do you think that means?

Knowledge is more than just an education. Knowledge means you have the power to look carefully at the world around you and decide if the things you see happening are right or wrong. When people do this, they can use their education and knowledge to change things that are wrong so that the world is better for everyone.

Today in the United States we have a system that provides free education for all children, no matter the color of their skin, the language they speak, whether they are rich, poor, or in the middle, and whatever their gender. It wasn't always that way! You probably know that a long time ago, women and girls were not given the same kind of education as boys and men. However, women weren't the only group of people to not have a fair chance at an education.

In the days of slavery, slaves were not allowed to learn how to read or write. The slave masters feared that if slaves were **literate** (able to read) they might rebel against them and demand freedom. Some people formed secret night schools to educate slaves. Some of these schools were called "pit schools" because they were actually holes in the ground deep in the woods, hidden from the slave masters. If the teachers were caught, they could be run out of town or even put in jail. There were stories of slaves who would hide books in their hats and whenever they found someone who was willing, would pull it out and ask them to help them learn to read.

When slavery ended, schools opened for the freed slaves. Some angry former slave owners would burn down the schools and try to stop the freed slaves from learning, but the schools were always rebuilt. The newly freed slaves wanted to have an education. They knew that with an education, you could do just about anything!

During the time when Jim Crow laws in the South were making life for African Americans so unfair, schools for African American children were not equal to the schools for white children. Children were forced to attend different schools. The schools for white children had better materials, books and teachers. Most of the schools for black children had old books that were hand-me-downs from the white schools. They had too many students and not enough teachers, desks, or chairs. Even worse, some schools in the South were not allowed to have books that included copies of the Constitution or Declaration of Independence. Some people were afraid that if the students saw these documents they would realize how unfair they were treated. The Declaration of Independence says that "all men are created equal" and some people were afraid if the African American students saw that the founders of the United States believed this, they could rebel and demand equal treatment.

Finally, in 1954, the Supreme Court decided that segregating schools was unfair and illegal. Soon, schools were open to all children regardless of the color of their skin. This was the first step of many to ensure that African American children would have just as many freedoms and opportunities as white children.

Education today still has many challenges. People with less money still often go to schools that are not as good as the children who come from families with more money. Some cities have schools that are wonderful in some neighborhoods, but terrible in other neighborhoods. This means that even in the same city, some children are getting a better education than children just a few miles away. There is still prejudice in our country and it hurts children and their chance at a great future. However, when you have knowledge, knowledge IS power. If you can spot something unfair or unjust in the world, you can use your great mind and your education to help fix things that are not fair.

All of us have the power to use our knowledge to help make the world a better place!

Comparison of a school for black children (right) and a school for white children (left) in the 1930s

## Illustrated by Brittany Goris

Brittany is an artist and educator who combines her passions in Girls Rock Math to help youth achieve their potential. She loves finding creative ways like her illustrations to teach kids about Mathematicians and role models in STEM fields. In her free time she likes to rock climb, play board games, and cook vegetarian meals.

## Written by Jessica Christianson

Jessica is a Washington native and loves living in the Pacific Northwest. She lives on Bainbridge Island with her young son, where they love to explore the local playgrounds, beaches, and hiking trails together on sunny days. Jessica, a former elementary school teacher, created the Girls Rock Math program to empower more girls to feel confident in math. Writing these books about inspiring women in the field of mathematics is one way she hopes to inspire young girls!

Made in the USA
Middletown, DE
10 September 2018